STARS OF
WOMEN'S
SOCCER

Abbeville Press Publishers
New York · London

A portion of the book's proceeds are donated to the **Hugo Bustamante AYSO Playership Fund**, a national scholarship program to help ensure that no child misses the chance to play AYSO Soccer. Donations to the fund cover the cost of registration and a uniform for a child in need.

Text by Illugi Jökulsson

For the original edition
Design: Ólafur Gunnar Guðlaugsson
Layout: Ólafur Gunnar Guðlaugsson and Árni Torfason

For the English-language edition
Editor: Nicole Lanctot
Production manager: Louise Kurtz
Layout: Ada Rodriguez
Copy editor: Mike O'Connor

PHOTOGRAPHY CREDITS

Getty Images: p. 6 (Laurence Griffiths), 10 (Grant Halverson), 12 (Michael Regan), 14 (Christof Koepsel), 17 (Oleg Nikishin), 20 (Otto Greule Jr), 25 (Jamie Sabau), 26 (Doug Pensinger), 29 (Srdjan Stevanovic/Bongarts), 30 (Michael Steele), 31 (Michael Regan), 33 (Dino Panato), 34 (Chung Sung-Jun), 36 (Al Bello), 38 (Brian Blanco), 40 (Filipe Farinha), 42 (Jeff Vinnick/Bongarts), 44 (Tom Dulat), 46 (Matt Trommer), 50 (Francis Bompard), 52 (Richard Heatcote), 54 (Christof Koepsel), 56 (Stanley Chou), 58 (Jonathan Ferrey), 60 (Jamie Squire)

Wikimedia Commons: p. 18 (Christopher Johnson), 48 (Jay Solomon)

Árni Torfason: p. 8, 23

First published in the United States of America in 2015 by Abbeville Press, 116 West 23rd Street, New York, NY 10011

First edition
10 9 8 7 6 5 4 3 2 1

Library of Congress Cataloging-in-Publication Data

Illugi Jvkulsson.
  Stars of women's soccer / by Illugi Jvkulsson. -- First edition.
    pages cm
  Audience: Age: 7.
  ISBN 978-0-7892-1238-2
  1. Women Soccer players--Biography--Juvenile literature. 2. Soccer for women--Juvenile literature.
  I. Title.
  GV944.9.A1I55 2015
  796.334092'2--dc23
  [B]
                                  2015013479

For bulk and premium sales and for text adoption procedures, write to Customer Service Manager, Abbeville Press, 116 West 23rd Street, New York, NY 10011, or call 1-800-ARTBOOK.

Visit Abbeville Press online at www.abbeville.com.

CONTENTS

CAMILLE ABILY	6	AYA MIYAMA	34
NADINE ANGERER	8	ALEX MORGAN	36
RAMONA BACHMANN	10	LOUISA NÉCIB	38
VERÓNICA BOQUETE	12	YŪKI ŌGIMI	40
NILLA FISCHER	14	ALEXANDRA POPP	42
LENA GOESSLING	16	CHRISTEN PRESS	44
LAUREN HOLIDAY	18	CHRISTINE RAMPONE	46
NAHOMI KAWASUMI	20	MEGAN RAPINOE	48
NADINE KESSLER	22	WENDIE RENARD	50
SYDNEY LEROUX	24	CÉLIA ŠAŠIC	52
CARLI LLOYD	26	LOTTA SCHELIN	54
DZSENIFER MAROZSÁN	28	CHRISTINE SINCLAIR	56
MARTA	30	HOPE SOLO	58
VIVIANNE MIEDEMA	32	ABBY WAMBACH	60

CAMILLE ABILY
MIDFIELDER
FRANCE

BORN DECEMBER 5, 1984
IN RENNES, FRANCE
HEIGHT 5'6"
CURRENT TEAM LYON (FRA)
INTERNATIONAL GAMES 120
GOALS 23

CAMILLE ABILY

The Versatile Midfielder

Camille Abily is one of the major pillars of the French national team, elevating them to the status of the world's greatest. In 2011, France came in fourth place at the Women's World Cup and a year later once again landed in fourth at the Summer Olympics in London. During the 2013 UEFA Women's Euro, the French team was disappointingly knocked out in the quarterfinal. As a result, Philippe Bergeroo was hired as manager to give the team a better opportunity at securing improved results in upcoming tournaments. The French team is definitely composed of the right stuff. Fierce forwards entered the stage, including Élodie Thomis, Marie-Laure Delie, and Eugénie Le Sommer.

Wendie Renard and Louisa Nécib control the play at midfield along with Abily, who is undoubtedly one of the world's best at the position. She is equally adept at running the attacking show and covering the defense.

Abily has played with a number of teams throughout her career but has remained with Lyon, in her home country, the longest. With Lyon, she has won six league titles, four cup titles, and twice won the UEFA Women's Champions League. Moreover, Abily has twice traveled to the United States and played for a short span, first with Los Angeles Sol and then with FC Gold Pride, both in the old Women's Professional Soccer league.

In the spring of 2015, Lyon clinched French league championship by winning their first 20 games! With this, Abily became the most triumphant woman in the history of French soccer. She has been French league champion ten times and French cup champion five times!

NADINE ANGERER

The German Goalkeeping Stalwart

Patience and perseverance characterize the career of the fantastic German goalkeeper Nadine Angerer. She won six major titles with the national team from 1997 to 2005 without playing a single game. She was always the second-string goalkeeper behind the powerful Silke Rottenberg, who never missed a game. Yet Angerer refused to complain; rather, she waited for her time to come. During those years, Angerer collected a host of awards with her club Turbine Potsdam and jumped at every opportunity to play with the national team. In 2007, she was chosen as Best Goalkeeper at the Women's World Cup after not conceding a single goal in six matches! Germany confidently defeated Brazil 2–0 in the final after the Brazilian powerhouse had crushed the U.S. national team 4–0 in the semifinal. There was no question that Angerer now counted among the world's leading goalkeepers, on par with Iceland's Thora Helgadottir and the United States' Hope Solo.

Angerer has played a big part in the German team's recent successes. She served as captain of the team after the fantastic Birgit Prinz retired in 2012 and led the Germans to victory at the 2013 UEFA Women's Euro. Angerer conceded only one goal in six matches throughout the tournament. The performance led to her being named FIFA World Player of the Year in 2014. She was the first goalkeeper, male or female, to be awarded that honor.

Angerer has played with the Portland Thorns since 2014, alongside American World Cup stars Tobin Heath and Alex Morgan and Canada's Christine Sinclair. During the 2007 Women's World Cup final against Brazil, Angerer defended a penalty kick from the genius Marta. And on the way to the 2013 Euro final, she managed to thwart two penalty kicks in the championship match.

NADINE ANGERER
GOALKEEPER
GERMANY

BORN NOVEMBER 10, 1978
IN LOHR, BAVARIA, GERMANY
HEIGHT 5'9"
CURRENT TEAM PORTLAND
THORNS (USA)
INTERNATIONAL GAMES 137

Cristiano Ronaldo and Nadine Angerer were chosen best players of 2013.

BORN DECEMBER 25, 1990
IN MALTERS, SWITZERLAND
HEIGHT 5'4"
CURRENT TEAM ROSENGARD
(SWE)
INTERNATIONAL GAMES 58
GOALS 32

RAMONA BACHMANN

Switzerland's Steadfast Future

Ramona Bachmann was born in a tiny village in the Swiss Alps with a population of 7,000. Her father was the coach of the village soccer team, so she grew up with a soccer ball at her feet. As a small child, Bachmann served as the team's mascot, and she later began training under the tutelage of her father. At just 16, she joined a team in the nearby city of Lucerne. Next, she traveled to Sweden, where she has played ever since, aside from a brief stint in the United States.

The Swiss national team has not traditionally been in the group of Europe's best, though recently the team has improved greatly, not least due to Bachmann's presence on the field.

Bachmann led the Swiss team in the qualifying stages for the 2015 Women's World Cup. The Swiss team features powerful strikers, and along with Bachmann, it is worth mentioning Ana Maria Crnogorčević and Lara Dickenmann. All three are powerful strikers and goal scorers; however, no one surpasses Bachmann when it comes to hunting goal opportunities and taking advantage of them. Bachmann is powerful and insightful, and she never gives up.

In a 2011 World Cup qualification match against England, Bachmann faked an injury and threw herself to the ground after brushing against the English goalkeeper. The referee fell for the trick and dismissed the goalkeeper. Bachmann would later apologize for her behavior, saying that she had allowed her competitive mood to lead her astray. Nowadays, there is no need for cheap antics; her skill has led to her being dubbed the "Swiss Magician."

VERÓNICA BOQUETE
FORWARD
SPAIN

BORN APRIL 9, 1987
IN SANTIAGO DE COMPOSTELA,
GALICIA, SPAIN
HEIGHT 5'3"
CURRENT TEAM FRANKFURT
(GER)
INTERNATIONAL GAMES 34
GOALS 24

VERÓNICA BOQUETE

Spain's Ball-Controlling Magician

Spain managed to win a seat at the final tournament of the 2015 Women's World Cup. This achievement followed another one, where the team participated in the 2013 UEFA Women's Euro and did incredibly well, reaching the quarterfinal. The national squad boasts a number of talented players, all of whom contribute to the ongoing success of the team. Among the standout players are forwards Sonia Bermúdez and Natalia Pablos. However, it is safe to say that no one has played a bigger part in Spain's upsurge than the fantastic Verónica Boquete.

Boquete entered the scene around the time when Spain clinched, to everyone's surprise, the 2004 UEFA Women's U-19 Championship, when she was only 17. A year later she began playing with the senior national team. Boquete is consistent and resourceful, and she has slowly but surely traveled the path toward becoming one the world's greatest female soccer players.

Boquete is not only a prolific goal scorer; she also produces an endless stream of assists for her teammates and wreaks havoc every time she has the ball.

Boquete has traveled widely during her career, playing in her home country as well as in Russia, Sweden, and the United States. In 2014, she joined the German team Frankfurt but hoped for a later return to the United States.

! Spaniards can't get enough of Boquete. She is Spain's first female soccer player to have a biography written about her. The book carries the very fitting title Vero Boquete: The Princess of the Majestic Game.

NILLA FISCHER

Fighting Spirit Embodied

Pia Sundhage was a legendary Swedish soccer player and a member of the Swedish national team for 21 years, from 1975 to 1996. Since retiring, Sundhage has utilized her extensive soccer experience in her coaching, serving, for example, as manager of the U.S. women's national team from 2007 to 2012. After winning two Olympic gold medals, Sundhage returned to Sweden and took over the helm of the Swedish national team. One of her first tasks was to transfer veteran defensive midfielder Nilla Fischer deeper on the field and give her the position of defender.

Fischer was close to 30, and her record with Sweden consisted of almost 100 international games at the midfield position. Fischer was a hard-tackling no-nonsense defensive player, but when Sundhage moved her to the heart of the defense, Fischer's career took an interesting turn.

Paradoxically, the move seemed to have a positive effect on Fischer's goal scoring. She scored three goals at the 2013 UEFA Women's Euro and was the second-place goal scorer in the tournament, behind only her teammate Lotta Schelin. First and foremost, Fischer was queen of her defensive empire for the Swedish team.

Fischer was for a while captain of the powerful Malmö team, in southern Sweden, but has played for the Swedish team Linköpings in recent years. In the summer of 2013, Fischer decided to change course and joined the fierce German club Wolfsburg, which had just snatched a celebrated triad: league and cup championships in Germany and a victory at the UEFA Women's Champions League. With Fischer on the team, Wolfsburg triumphantly defended the German championship title and once again took home the Champions League crown.

Fischer is a true Swede. She routinely visits the IKEA near Wolfsburg, where they sell Swedish meatballs . . .

NILLA FISCHER
DEFENDER
SWEDEN

BORN AUGUST 2, 1984
IN VERUM, SWEDEN
HEIGTH 5'9"
CURRENT TEAM WOLFSBURG
(GER)
INTERNATIONAL GAMES 122
GOALS 18

LENA GOESSLING

The Dynamic Midfielder

Public soccer games featuring women players were officially banned in Germany from 1955 until 1970! However, after the ban was lifted, Germany quickly rose through the ranks and became one of the world's greatest teams. The German women's team won the World Cup both in 2003 and 2007, and they snatched the UEFA European Women's Championship title an amazing eight times—of which six were consecutive, from 1995 to 2013! Nevertheless, for the better part of the twenty-first century, Germany has sat in second on the FIFA ranking list, but they managed to clinch the first-place ranking in December 2014.

Germany's center is tremendously dynamic. There, Nadine Kessler reigns supreme, but the vigorous Lena Goessling is no less of a stalwart presence. When she is out on the pitch, her technical prowess, speed, and powerful shots never fail to impress. She is fast and gifted and has good technique. Whenever the German national team enters a match, Goessling's responsibilities are many, and her contributions are decisive. Goessling has played with the powerhouse club Wolfsburg in her home country and won the German league title twice, the German Cup once, and the UEFA Women's Champions League twice. She also became European champion with the German national team in 2013. The Germans played six games and lost only one of them. It is no coincidence that Goessling was absent from the losing match, due to minor injuries.

Despite playing her first international game with Germany in 2008, Goessling was not named to the German squad for the 2008 Summer Olympics or the 2009 UEFA Women's Euro. She was, however, chosen for the team that played in the 2011 Women's World Cup, and since then she hasn't missed a game with Germany in any major tournament.

LENA GOESSLING
MIDFIELDER
GERMANY

BORN MARCH 8, 1986
IN BIELEFELD, GERMANY
HEIGHT 5'7"
CURRENT TEAM WOLFSBURG
(GER)
INTERNATIONAL GAMES 71
GOALS 8

LAUREN HOLIDAY
MIDFIELDER
UNITED STATES

BORN SEPTEMBER 30, 1987
IN INDIANAPOLIS, INDIANA,
UNITED STATES
HEIGHT 5'8"
CURRENT TEAM KANSAS CITY
(USA)
INTERNATIONAL GAMES 119
GOALS 23

"I get nervous all the time about not making the team," said Holiday. "Each level is like climbing a pyramid, and the national team is the absolute highest point. There's thunder pressure . . . to win and perform every single day . . . I want to be a better soccer player, and whether I make the team or not I want to train as hard as I can."

LAUREN HOLIDAY

The Playmaker

The U.S. women's national team has remained on top of the FIFA ranking list for most of the twenty-first century. Ferocious forwards from Mia Hamm to Abby Wambach have probably had the most obvious part to play in this ongoing success, but credit must also be given to the team's sturdy and unwavering midfielders. Ever since her first appearance in an international game in 2007, Lauren Holiday has proven an indispensable contributor for bringing force, attacking spirit, and oversight to the midfield play. Holiday, who bore the last name Cheney until her marriage in 2013, was born with a heart defect, which was corrected by means of open-heart surgery when she was three years old. The operation was a success, and Holiday turned into a fantastic athlete.

On the soccer pitch, she tirelessly seeks to advance her team, create goal opportunities, and maintain control of the play. She is a precision shot, and when Holiday fires a ball toward the goal, opponents tremble, because few strikers on the U.S. team are as precise as her. This ability has led to her scoring copious amounts of goals from a distance. She is fearless when it comes to taking initiative, and her teammates frequently turn to her when the going gets tough. Furthermore, few players on the national team contribute the number of assists that she does.

Veteran Shannon Boxx is still in top form at midfield, and players such as Tobin Heath are gaining prominence, but Holiday still deserves recognition as the U.S. team's major playmaker.

NAHOMI KAWASUMI
FORWARD
JAPAN

BORN SEPTEMBER 23, 1985
IN YAMATO, KANAGAWA, JAPAN
HEIGHT 5'2"
CURRENT TEAM SEATTLE REIGN
(USA)
INTERNATIONAL GAMES 67
GOALS 18

NAHOMI KAWASUMI

All-Around Artist

The 2011 Women's World Cup was held in Germany, and fans and pundits generally assumed that the U.S. team would battle the host nation for the championship, given the fact that both teams had for a time been a cut above other women's national teams. Moreover, the consensus seemed to be that Brazil, Sweden, and France were most likely to provide some challenge to the two favorites. However, strange things happened. Japan's team, which had never before advanced past the Women's World Cup quarterfinals, was surprisingly victorious. Led by the fantastic Homare Sawa, the team kicked out Germany and Sweden during the knockout stage and went on to win the final in a celebrated victory over the United States in a penalty shootout. A year later, the Japanese national team proved that their world champion title was no fluke by reaching the gold medal game at the 2012 Summer Olympics in London. The U.S. team, however, got their revenge that time and took home the gold. Homare has recently begun slowing down her pace, and Kawasumi is now the main pillar of the Japanese national team. In fact, Kawasumi has remained one of the most powerful forwards on the team since she joined in 2008. She is small and appears delicate at first sight, but she is lightning quick and agile, and she scores and assists goals with great style.

As well as being recognizable on the field with her thin pink headband, Kawasumi has attracted attention for her unusual talents off the field. She has great interest in fingernail art and often paints her nails before matches with beautiful images and patterns.

Kawasumi began her senior career in Japan with INAC Kobe Leonessa. The name means "lioness" in Italian. The reason why this Japanese club chose an Italian name is unclear, but Kawasumi and her companions proved to be true competitors: when Japan won the 2011 World Cup, the team featured seven lionesses from Kobe.

NADINE KESSLER

Team Captain!

Nadine Kessler served in the German army and reached the rank of corporal. She also completed studies in health management. Kessler joined the powerful team Wolfsburg in 2011, adopting the position of team captain. She led the team to three major victories in 2013: both the German league and cup championships as well as the title in the UEFA Women's Champions League. She became European champion the same year with the German national team. In 2014, Kessler once again led Wolfsburg's team to the league championship and Champions League glory.

Kessler is a driven midfielder, unyielding fighter, and loyal to Wolfsburg, simply exclaiming, "I love my team."

Kessler won the 2013 UEFA Women's Euro with the German national team and was a year later the recipient of the UEFA Best Women's Player in Europe Award. She arrived at the high summit of her career in early 2015, when she was awarded the 2014 FIFA World Player of the Year Award. She collected her honor with Cristiano Ronaldo, who won the same award in the male category.

Kessler and Ronaldo accept their FIFA World Player of the Year awards in early 2015.

NADINE KESSLER
ATTACKING MIDFIELDER
GERMANY

BORN APRIL 4, 1988
IN LANDSTUHL, GERMANY
HEIGHT 5'7"
CURRENT TEAM WOLFSBURG
(GER)
INTERNATIONAL GAMES 29
GOALS 10

SYDNEY LEROUX

The Competitor

Even though Sydney Leroux was born in Canada to a Canadian mother, early on she decided that she wanted to join the U.S. national team and play for her American father's homeland. She was only 15 when she journeyed alone to Arizona, where she went to school and played soccer. Leroux had at that point already played for the senior club team in Vancouver, Canada, and had played in two matches for the Canadian U-19 team.

Leroux claims that moving to the States was a difficult trial; however, she was determined, and soon she was making a name for herself in American soccer. She joined the U.S. national team at only 21 years old, and there she has flourished.

She averages a goal in every other game. In January 2012, she scored five goals during an Olympic qualifying match against Guatemala, despite entering the match in the second half. Interestingly enough, her teammate Amy Rodriguez had also scored five goals in the second half of a game against the Dominican Republic.

There is no doubt that Leroux's fighting spirit and skillfulness will be of good use to the U.S. national team in the future. Manager Jillian Ellis says that Leroux is the "most competitive person I've worked with, mentally and physically. She's been through a lot. When it's harder for her . . . she's better."

Leroux played many sports when she was young. Said Leroux, "My mom literally put me in every sport possible growing up because I had crazy energy, and she thought that if I had three different practices to go to a day, I would eventually get tired. Needless to say, that never worked."

SYDNEY LEROUX
STRIKER
UNITED STATES

BORN MAY 7, 1990
IN SURREY, BRITISH
COLUMBIA, CANADA
HEIGHT 5'7"
CURRENT TEAM WESTERN
NEW YORK FLASH (USA)
INTERNATIONAL GAMES 66
GOALS 33

CARLI LLOYD

The Midfield Goal–Scoring Machine

Carli Lloyd's role on the U.S. national team is not intended to be that of major goal scorer. She plays midfield and is first and foremost supposed to transfer the ball from the defense to the offense, where the ball is received by Alex Morgan, Christen Press, or Abby Wambach. However, on a strong and balanced team such as the American one, everyone has opportunities to score, and Lloyd has definitely taken advantage of those opportunities. She is the all-time leading goal-scoring midfielder on the team and averages a goal every third game. In fact, Lloyd will probably always be remembered for her winning goals in two Olympic gold medal games in a row.

During the final at the 2008 Beijing Olympics, the U.S. team had to face the offensively talented Brazilian team. They managed to hold the Brazilians back, but the U.S. team also needed to score goals. The game was extended, and Lloyd positioned herself just outside the penalty area, finally smashing the ball into the net from a long shot. The goal clinched the medal for the U.S. team.

Four years later, in London, it was uncertain as to whether Lloyd would be a member of the starting team. However, due to the injury of a teammate, Lloyd joined and gave a fantastic performance. After scoring two goals in the group stage, she was a jack-of-all-trades in the final against the Japanese world champions. First, Lloyd scored off a header, on an assist from Morgan, and then on her second goal, she dashed 25 yards through the center and blasted the ball into the net with a beautiful long shot.

Lloyd was then the top goal scorer at an important tournament in Brazil in December 2014, with five goals in four matches. And during the strenuous Algarve Cup in March 2015, Lloyd scored both goals in a 2–1 victory over the powerful Norwegian team. Lloyd continued to prove that she is one of the most lethal weapons on the U.S. national team.

! The members of the U.S. women's national team are becoming increasingly famous in their country. They are often featured on the covers of fashion and glamour magazines and appear on TV programs. Lloyd and some of her teammates even made an appearance on *The Daily Show with Jon Stewart*.

CARLI LLOYD
MIDFIELDER
UNITED STATES

BORN JULY 16, 1982
IN DEIRAN, NEW JERSEY,
UNITED STATES
HEIGHT 5'9"
CURRENT TEAM HOUSTON
DASH (USA)
INTERNATIONAL GAMES 190
GOALS 63

DZSENIFER MAROZSÁN

The Past and the Future

János Marozsán was for time a member of the Hungarian national team. In 1996, he joined the soccer club Saarbrücken in Germany, and his four-year-old daughter, Dzsenifer, sometimes accompanied him to practice. Before long, it was clear that the young Marozsán was a tremendously gifted soccer player. She joined neighboring youth teams and played only with boys early on. The family decided to stay in Germany, and Marozsán became the youngest ever player in Germany's top league, the Bundesliga, playing her first game at the age of 14. Moreover, she also holds the record for being the youngest player to score a goal in the Bundesliga, at only 15 years 4 months. In October 2010, she played in her first national game for Germany, at age 18.

Marozsán is a classic attacking midfielder with a sharp sense for cooperation. She continuously seeks out goal opportunities and has numerous goals under her belt. Marozsán has scored roughly a goal every other match with the national team. She is one of the youngest members of the German team's starting lineup, and given that her talents as a soccer player have yet to peak, one can assume that she will count among the world's greatest female soccer players for years to come.

Marozsán is a serious dog lover, and she has this little princess, who is her pride and joy.

DZSENIFER MAROZSÁN
ATTACKING MIDFIELDER
GERMANY

BORN APRIL 18, 1992
IN BUDAPEST, HUNGARY
HEIGHT 5'7
CURRENT TEAM FRANKFURT
(GER)
INTERNATIONAL GAMES 46
GOALS 22

MARTA

International Star

It is incredible that Marta Vieira da Silva will not reach the age of 30 until 2016, because she has been a household name in the world of women's soccer for what seems like ages. Marta's fame has in fact spread way beyond the confines of soccer fandom. In 2004, she came in third on the list for FIFA World Player of the Year. Only the legends Brigit Prinz and Mia Hamm managed to surpass the 18-year-old from Brazil. Finally, in 2006, Marta collected the title for the first time, and then she repeated for the next four years in a row! Since 2011, she has landed in either third or second place each year.

Marta has led the Brazilian offense in numerous big tournaments, racking up goals and accumulating a host of individual awards. And Brazilians are aching to witness their favorite star clinch the highest honor of all: a world championship.

Marta is a tremendously gifted goal scorer and has a razor-sharp eye for technique and teamwork. Moreover, she is sometimes compared to her legendary countryman Pelé.

Marta has played in the United States a number of times in her career, but she has mostly played for clubs in Sweden, where women's soccer is highly respected.

Argentina's Lionel Messi and Brazil's Marta were each named FIFA World Player of the Year in 2012.

MARTA
STRIKER
BRAZIL

BORN FEBRUARY 19, 1986
OM DOIS RIACHOS, ALAGOAS,
BRAZIL
HEIGHT 5'3"
CURRENT TEAM ROSENGARD
(SWE)
INTERNATIONAL GAMES 96
GOALS 86

VIVIANNE MIEDEMA

The Biggest Talent?

The Dutch women's national team played their first international match in 1973, and for a long time the team achieved little success. However, the tides have turned in recent years. In 2009, the Netherlands participated in their first major tournament, entering the final rounds of the UEFA Women's Euro and surprisingly finishing in third place. And in 2015, the Dutch qualified for their first Women's World Cup final tournament.

A major part of the Dutch team's upswing can be attributed to Manon Melis, a fierce goal scorer who has manned the front line of the team for more than a decade. And the team has acquired further promising forwards recently, for example the left winger/forward Lieke Martens.

However, a young forward has also entered the scene: Vivianne Miedema, a towering player who racks up goals for the national team. Many believe that she soon will number among the world's top female forwards. Miedema is a modest player known for celebrating her numerous goals in an almost laconic way. Her goals come in all colors of the rainbow.

"Right foot, left foot—it is all the same to me. I just shoot with whichever foot is nearest," said Miedema. Commenting on her cool demeanor after a goal, she told the website UEFA.com: "Of course I am happy, but I'm a bit down to earth and celebrate a bit less enthusiastically than the others. That's just me."

Miedema will be 18 years old during the 2015 Women's World Cup, and many soccer fans look forward to watching this powerful striker develop.

Bayern Munich has a leading position in men's soccer, counting a number of superstars, such as Arjen Robben, among its ranks. Miedema has been given the task of raising the women's team to the same status. She retweeted this image of herself with Robben.

VIVIANNE MIEDEMA
FORWARD
NETHERLANDS

BORN JULY 15, 1996
IN HOOGEVEEN, NETHERLANDS
HEIGHT 5'8"
CURRENT TEAM BAYERN
MUNICH (GER)
INTERNATIONAL GAMES 18
GOALS 18

AYA MIYAMA
MIDFIELDER
JAPAN

BORN JANUARY 28, 1985
IN AMISHIRASATO, CHIBA,
JAPAN
HEIGHT 5'2"
CURRENT TEAM OKAYAMA
YUNOGO BELLE (JPN)
INTERNATIONAL GAMES 144
GOALS 34

34

AYA MIYAMA

The Role Model

As explained on page 21, the Japanese team was surprisingly triumphant at the 2011 Women's World Cup, as they beat the United States in the final, having knocked out the powerful national teams from Sweden and Germany earlier in the tournament. The genius Homare Sawa played the most significant role, but Aya Miyama also contributed greatly to the team's startling success. Miyama scored the first goal in the penalty shootout that would determine the victor following a 2–2 draw in the final. Miyama had also scored one of the goals during the match itself, just before the end of the normal game time. She also assisted on a goal by Sawa that equalized the game right before extra time was to end.

Following the penalty shootout, which the Japanese women won by a score of 3–1, Miyama did not participate in her team's celebration but instead first went over to the dismayed American players and hugged them and thanked them for their noble sportsmanship and congratulated them for their overall performance in the tournament.

Her behavior clearly showed that Miyama is not just an incredibly skilled and creative midfielder, equipped with great oversight and an eye for both offense and defense; she is also a true sportsman.

The Japanese national team has maintained its winning streak, and in May 2014, Miyama captained the team on its way to its first AFC Women's Asian Cup title by defeating Australia. A team that has Aya Miyama on board need not fear, and when such a team also boasts players such as Nahomi Kawasumi, Yuki Ogimi, and even the veteran Sawa, they become a formidable and worthy foe for any opponent.

Miyama scored the winning goal—a beautiful free kick—in Japan's victory over New Zealand at the 2011 Women's World Cup in Germany. She also scored the team's first goal in the final against the United States. In addition, Miyama scored Japan's first penalty of the penalty shootout, helping lead her team to victory.

ALEX MORGAN

The Game Winner

In her youth, Alex Morgan was called the "Baby Horse" because of both her lightning-quick running speed and her diligence and dexterity. And even though the nickname didn't stick, the characteristics of Morgan as a soccer player still remain the same. Morgan was long considered the worthy heir to daring striker Abby Wambach on the front lines of the U.S. national team, and it is now clear that Morgan is the team's major striker. Morgan is not solely a goal scorer; she also eagerly assists Wambach's and other teammates' goals.

Morgan is widely known as an all-around talent. For example, she has published a series of novels for young readers that revolve around a group of young girls who play soccer.

Morgan recorded a goal and an assist in the 2011 Women's World Cup final against Japan. It was the first time ever that an American player had accomplished that feat. She was a pillar on the team that avenged the harrowing World Cup defeat and steamrolled the Japanese team for the gold medal at the 2012 Summer Olympics. That year was Morgan's greatest year so far with the national team; she played 31 games, scored 28 goals, and made

Morgan has become one of the United States' most famous female soccer players and was among a group invited to meet First Lady Michelle Obama at the White House.

BORN JULY 2, 1989
IN DIAMOND BAR, NEAR LOS
ANGELES, CALIFORNIA,
UNITED STATES
HEIGHT 5'7"
CURRENT TEAM PORTLAND
THORNS (USA)
INTERNATIONAL GAMES 82
GOALS 51

LOUISA NÉCIB
MIDFIELDER
FRANCE

BORN JANUARY 23, 1987
IN MARSEILLE, FRANCE
HEIGHT 5'6"
CURRENT TEAM LYON (FRA)
INTERNATIONAL GAMES 123
GOALS 32

LOUISA NÉCIB

The Unpredictable Genius

In France, Zinedine Zidane is generally acknowledged as an almost godlike soccer player. Not only did he lead France toward their only world championship title in 1998, but his skill and intelligence for the game are near unprecedented in history. Consequently, being compared to Zidane is no small thing, but such has been the case with Louisa Nécib. In fact, their similarity does not solely revolve around soccer talent; Zidane and Nécib both hail from the French city of Marseille and both have Algerian heritage. Nécib practiced gymnastics in her youth but played soccer in the streets with the neighborhood boys. When she discovered that there were special women's soccer teams, she began intense training, and her talents were immediately detectable. Since 2007, Nécib has played for the forceful Lyon team and has accumulated all accolades possible with a European soccer club, winning the French league championship seven times, the French Cup four times, and the UEFA Women's Champions League twice.

Nécib can play all midfield positions and often joins the offensive play. She plays as a winger on the French national team and as a playmaker with Lyon. Her vision and passing, which are described as "sublime," complement both positions. Both her understanding and her technique are top-notch, and former national team manager Bruno Bini has said of her: "Louisa is a very rare player. What she does, it's not in the textbooks. She is an artist. It's sunny when she touches the ball. She radiates the whole team."

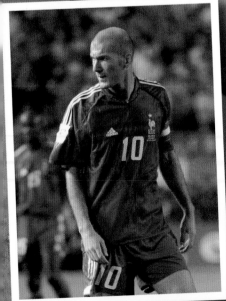

Louisa Nécib is often compared to Zinedine Zidane, who was one of the best players in the world from 1995 to 2005.

YŪKI ŌGIMI

Dexterity and Character

Yūki Ōgimi comes from a family of soccer players hailing from the city of Atsugi, near Yokohama, Japan. Ōgimi's older brother was a powerful soccer player who had played for a host of teams in Japan and Thailand. Her younger sister, Asano Nagasato, has played with the Japanese national team and is now a member of the German team Turbine Potsdam.

In the beginning, she played side by side with her older sister on the same club. Ōgimi was the top scorer in the German women's league that same year. Ōgimi's path took her to England next, where she played briefly with Chelsea. The English league is not as strong as the German one, so Ōgimi returned to Germany early in 2015 in order to polish her skill for the 2015 Women's World Cup.

She now plays with the German powerhouse Wolfsburg. Ōgimi was only 16 when she played in her first national game, in 2004. Her focus and fighting spirit were clear even in her youth, and she has developed into a potent and elegant striker. As a younger player, she would commonly stay after formal training was over to practice passing and long shots after her teammates had gone home. This diligence has characterized her ever since and aided her in reaching her goals.

Wolfsburg coach Ralf Kellermann was very happy to have this player join his team in 2015. He said, "We have managed to acquire a real goal threat and an international attacker."

YŪKI ŌGIMI
FORWARD
JAPAN

BORN JUNE 15, 1987
IN ATSUGI, KANAGAWA, JAPAN
HEIGHT 5'6"
CURRENT TEAM WOLFSBURG
(GER)
INTERNATIONAL GAMES 110
GOALS 50

ALEXANDRA POPP
ATTACKING MIDFIELDER
GERMANY

BORN APRIL 6, 1991
IN WITTGEN, GERMANY
HEIGHT 5'2"
CURRENT TEAM WOLFSBURG
(GER)
INTERNATIONAL GAMES 52
GOALS 27

Popp was the star of the German team that won the 2010 U-20 Women's World Cup in Germany. She was awarded the Golden Ball as the best player of the tournament and was also the top goal scorer. She achieved the near unprecedented feat of scoring in each of her team's six games, amassing ten goals.

ALEXANDRA POPP

Midfielder, Psychologist, and Zookeeper

Alexandra Popp attended an unusual school in her youth, Gesamtschule Berger Feld in the city of Gelsenkirchen, Germany. The school is one of the nation's four "elite schools of soccer" and is run by the German Football Association. The school is usually populated by promising boys, and the young Popp had to obtain a special permit to be able to attend. Popp studied and trained with junior players of the German men's Bundesliga team Schalke 04. Some of the school's students around the same age as Popp are the world-famous Mesut Özil, Benedikt Höwedes, and Julian Draxler. Unsurprisingly for a girl raised among soccer-playing boys, Popp's style is characterized by power and determination. She is strong, cunning, and versatile, and she is a true jack-of-all-trades, though she often gravitates toward the opponents' goal. Lately, Popp has played with Wolfsburg, but she will also be a prominent presence on the front lines of the stalwart German national team. When Popp finally retires from soccer, inactivity will not be among her fears. She has a degree in physiotherapy and is an educated zookeeper as well.

CHRISTEN PRESS

Tenacious Goal Scorer

There is no lack of young and aggressive forwards on the U.S. national team. Along with Alex Morgan and Sydney Leroux, Christen Press has also made a name for herself in recent years. Press played for Stanford University in her home state of California, becoming the all-time leading scorer for the women's soccer team, and many of her records still stand. In 2011, she joined magicJack of the Women's Professional Soccer league in the United States. That year she was named the league's Rookie of the Year, following a season in which she became the first-ever rookie to score a hat trick.

Press then journeyed to Sweden, where she played with strong clubs and racked up goals. The call from the U.S. national team was finally received in 2013, and Press is gaining prominence as one of the world's fiercest strikers.

Press is the all-time leading scorer for the Stanford University women's soccer team with 71 goals. While playing for the Cardinal, she broke all sorts of team records, including the record for the fastest goal: she scored only 37 seconds into a game against Sacramento State.

CHRISTEN PRESS
STRIKER
UNITED STATES

BORN DECEMER 29, 1988
IN LOS ANGELES, CALIFORNIA,
UNITED STATES
HEIGHT 5'7"
CURRENT TEAM CHICAGO RED
STARS (USA)
INTERNATIONAL GAMES 39
GOALS 19

CHRISTINE RAMPONE
DEFENDER
UNITED STATES

BORN JUNE 24, 1975
ON FORT LAUDERDALE,
FLORIDA, UNITED STATES
HEIGHT 5'6"
CURRENT TEAM SKY BLUE
(USA)
INTERNATIONAL GAMES 304
GOALS 4

CHRISTINE RAMPONE

The World's Most Seasoned Player

Christie Rampone will celebrate her 40th birthday during the 2015 Women's World Cup in Canada. Rampone was a member of the heralded U.S. national team that came out victorious, on their home field at the 1999 World Cup. Even though she made only one appearance during that tournament, the experience of mingling with American legends such as Mia Hamm, Michelle Akers, and Brandi Chastain, among others, turned out to be priceless for the young Rampone. She is now a legend in her own right and remains unruffled. Though she is not as quick as she used to be, she makes up for the shortcoming with extensive experience, incredible oversight, and passion, the latter of which has not diminished throughout her career. Rampone admits that this fighting spirit is her most valuable weapon.

Rampone ranks second on the all-time international games played list, following only Kristine Lilly, who played 352 games in a career stretching 23 years. Below Rampone on the list are companions from the famous 1999 team: Mia Hamm, Julie Foudy, and Joy Fawcett. They have all played more international games than the most capped male player. On top of the men's list is the Egyptian midfielder Ahmed Hassan, with 184 games.

The U.S. national team boasts a number of great defenders, including Becky Sauerbrunn and Rachel Van Hollebeke. Rampone still has much to offer this strong defensive core.

Rampone was a four-sport athlete at Point Pleasant Borough High School in New Jersey, competing in soccer, basketball, track and field, and field hockey. She received all-state honors in soccer, basketball, and field hockey and was the first athlete to lead her conference in scoring in all three sports.

MEGAN RAPINOE
MIDFIELDER
UNITED STATES

BORN JULY 5, 1985
IN REDDING, CALIFORNIA,
UNITED STATES
HEIGHT 5'7"
CURRENT TEAM SEATTLE REIGN
(USA)
INTERNATIONAL GAMES 98
GOALS 29

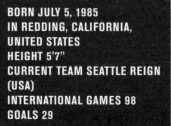

MEGAN RAPINOE

Unpredictable and Striking

Megan Rapinoe's trademark short blonde hair always make her recognizable on the field, but her skills as a crafty winger and cunning shot are the characteristics that truly define her as a soccer player. Rapinoe grew up in a family of athletes and began playing soccer at a young age with her twin sister, Megan.

Rapinoe showed promise from the start. For a time, it seemed like she would be forced to quit soccer due to injuries. Yet Rapinoe fully recovered and claims that the injuries toughened her as a player. She was a dominating presence at the 2011 Women's World Cup, scoring one goal and adding three assists, all of which led to important goals. Among other things, Rapinoe entered as a defender and made a razor-sharp pass to Abby Wambach who scored to tie the game in the the 122nd minute of an extended match against Brazil. When the game went to a penalty shootout, Rapinoe was one of the goal scorers who led the U.S. team to victory. Rapinoe added an assist on Alex Morgan's goal in the final, but the U.S. team was forced to settle for the second place following a losing effort to Japan.

During the 2012 Summer Olympics, Rapinoe's performance was even more prominent: she scored three goals in the tournament, two of which helped the U.S. team win a 4–3 victory over Canada in a famous semifinal match.

Along with Heather O'Reilly, Rapinoe is the fiercest winger on the U.S. national team. She is a colorful and enthusiastic soccer player, and her skills are numerous.

"The most un-American player in U.S. women's soccer, and that's a compliment. For decades the U.S. has thrived on strength and speed more than skill. Rapinoe is different. Rapinoe relies instead on clever dribbling, fluid movement, and visionary passing." —Grant Wahl, *Sports Illustrated*

Wendie Renard scuffles with Lotta Schelin from Sweden during the Olympic games in London on August 3, 2012. The two are teammates in Lyon, but here they are no holds barred in a heated international match.

WENDIE RENARD

Crafty Powerhouse

Wendie Renard was born on the island Martinique, a semiautonomous region of France located in the Caribbean. The island has an area of 436 square miles and a population of around 386,000. Renard began her soccer career with a local team in Martinique and played mainly with boys in her youth, and she became strong and tall at a young age. Around the age of 16, she moved to France to pursue the sport and joined the club Olympique Lyonnais, which is commonly known as Lyon. With Renard, the team has become French champion in eight consecutive years, won the French Cup four times, and twice won the UEFA Women's Champions League. Renard is team captain of Lyon despite her young age.

During the 2011 Champions League final, Renard scored the first of Lyon's two goals in a 2–0 victory over Turbine Potsdam from Germany. Renard's height and strength have an obvious part to play in her success, but she is first and foremost endowed with great technical skill and cunning. She mostly plays central defender but will sometimes enthusiastically engage in offensive play. Her grace on the field is always a delight to watch.

Renard will be one of the major faces of the 2016 UEFA Women's Euro in France. She often visits schools and discusses her life, background, and love of soccer.

WENDIE RENARD
DEFENDER
FRANCE

BORN JULY 20, 1990
IN SCHŒLCHER, MARTINIQUE
HEIGHT 6'1"
CURRENT TEAM LYON (FRA)
INTERNATIONAL GAMES 60
GOALS 16

CÉLIA ŠAŠIC
FORWARD
GERMANY

BORN JUNE 27, 1988
IN BONN, GERMANY
HEIGHT 5'9"
CURRENT TEAM FRANKFURT
(GER)
INTERNATIONAL GAMES 102
GOALS 56

CÉLIA ŠAŠIC

Veteran Goal Scorer

Célia Šašic is the perfect example of the contemporary multicultural Europe—and Germany in particular. Her father comes from Cameroon and her mother from France. She was a French citizen until the age of 15, despite being born in Germany. She then obtained German citizenship so she would be able to play with German youth teams, and a year later, in 2005, Šašic played her first match with the German senior national team.

She is a particularly daring forward and a zealous goal scorer, as good as unstoppable. Her family name is Okoyino da Mbabi, but she adopted the name Šašic after marrying a Croatian soccer player, Marko Šašic.

On November 19, 2011, Šašic scored four goals in a game against Kazakhstan during the qualifying stages for the 2013 UEFA Women's Euro. Her teammate Alexandra Popp also scored four goals. Teammates scoring four goals apiece in the same match is an exceptionally rare occurrence. Three games later, Šašic once again scored four goals in a game, this time against Spain. That time, Popp only managed one goal! And if that's not enough, Šašic repeated the move again, scoring four goals against Switzerland! In total, she scored 17 goals in seven games during the qualifying stages.

Šašic's goal-scoring abilities are constantly improving, and she is quickly becoming one of Europe's top goal scorers. On April 19, 2015, Frankfurt beat the Danish team Brønd 7–0 in their first match during the qualifying rounds for the UEFA Women's Champions League. Šašic scored four goals, an achievement that few players have managed in a qualifying match.

LOTTA SCHELIN
STRIKER/WINGER
SWEDEN

BORN FEBRUARY 27, 1984
IN TRANGSUND, SWEDEN
HEIGHT 5'11"
CURRENT TEAM LYON (FRA)
INTERNATIONAL GAMES 145
GOALS 75

LOTTA SCHELIN

The Resourceful Forward

As an adolescent, Lotta Schelin developed back pains and went to see a doctor. The doctor informed her that she had a problem with her spine and advised her to immediately cease playing soccer, because the sport could irreversibly damage her health. Schelin did not like the sound of this. She was extremely interested in sports and had for long dabbled in table tennis, track and field, and snowboarding. And now Schelin decided that she wanted to make a career out of soccer, despite being small for her age and fragile. Schelin's older sister, Camilla, was her role model in this regard, the latter being an accomplished soccer player.

Lotta couldn't imagine giving up soccer, and through intense physical training, she finally managed to overcome her back problems. And as she grew taller and stronger, a tremendously talented soccer player appeared—a powerful striker or a daring attacking winger.

In 2008, Schelin was invited to play in the United States but instead chose to join the burgeoning women's soccer scene in France. There, Schelin flourishes and scores almost one goal per game.

She has won the French league championship six times, twice won the cup championship, and twice won the UEFA Women's Champions League title. Moreover, as an individual Schelin has collected numerous awards.

Schelin played her first international match when she was 20 years old and is now at the high point of her career with the team, which has for long counted among the world's greatest.

Forward Sofia Jakobsson has recently proven herself as a major asset to the powerful Swedish national team. However, Schelin is not intimidated by younger players. In April 2015, Schelin carried Lyon into the final of the French Cup against Montpellier and scored the winning goal shortly after Montpellier had equalized the game, showing that anything can be expected from her at the World Cup!

CHRISTINE SINCLAIR
FORWARD
CANADA

BORN JUNE 12, 1983
IN BURNABY, BRITISH
COLUMBIA, CANADA
HEIGHT 5'9"
CURRENT TEAM PORTLAND
THORNS (USA)
INTERNATIONAL GAMES 214
GOALS 214

CHRISTINE SINCLAIR

Relentless Goal Scorer

Christine Sinclair is by far the greatest Canadian soccer player ever. Sinclair comes from a long line of athletes, and it was clear from early on that she would become a fierce goal scorer and versatile forward. Sinclair journeyed to the United States and studied at the University of Portland, winning all possible kinds of accolades and breaking numerous records during her college career. At 20, Sinclair played a big part in Canada's surprising success at the 2003 Women's World Cup, helping the team to a fourth-place finish. The Canadian team lost the third-place match to their U.S. neighbors. The U.S. team featured legends Mia Hamm and Kristine Lilly as well as young players who are now in their top form, namely, Abby Wambach and Christie Rampone. The final score of the match was 3–1, and Sinclair scored the lone goal for Canada.

The Canadian team reached even further at the 2012 Summer Olympics in London. With Sinclair at the helm, the team made it all the way to the semifinal and played fantastically. Sinclair managed to gain an advantage over the U.S. team three times with a hat trick of elegant goals, but the U.S. squad equalized every time, and Alex Morgan finally netted the winning goal for the United States in injury time. Devastated, Sinclair accused the referee of favoring the American team with a few controversial decisions. She had to pay a fine for the disagreeable comments but completed the Olympics as the top goal-scorer with six goals on the way to the Canadian team taking home the bronze medal.

Sinclair is now in third place on the list of all-time international goals scored by either male or female soccer players. Only her neighbors and rivals Abby Wambach and Mia Hamm have scored more goals than her.

When Sinclair started playing soccer, it was not love at first sight. Her brother introduced her to the sport when she was four and she played on a team with eight-year-olds. "She was tiny and it wasn't fun. But as she got into it and got older, she decided soccer was the way she was going to go."

BORN JULY 30, 1981
IN RICHLAND, WASHINGTON,
UNITED STATES
HEIGHT 5'9"
CURRENT TEAM SEATTLE REIGN
(USA)
INTERNATIONAL GAMES 165

HOPE SOLO

Colorful Character

Hope Solo, goalkeeper for the U.S. national team, is a very controversial person off the playing field. Solo has a fierce temper and often gets into trouble, both through words and actions, and she seems to have a slight problem with authority. She described her upbringing, which was quite unusual, in her autobiography, *Solo: A Memoir of Hope.* There and elsewhere, Hope admitted that she has often struggled with controlling her temper, which her life story clearly shows.

However, the story of Hope Solo the soccer player is a different one. Solo is simply a magnificent goalkeeper and serves her team with dignity and honor. She played a significant role in securing the U.S. team's gold medal at the 2008 Beijing Olympics, gloriously defending one shot after another from Marta and other dynamic Brazilian forwards. At the 2011 Women's World Cup, Solo was selected as the Golden Glove winner for best goalkeeper of the tournament. During the 2012 Summer Olympics, she was like an impenetrable wall in the goal throughout the final against Japan, eventually clinching the gold medal for the U.S. team. Solo's goalkeeping in the penalty shootout in the 2015 Algarve Cup championship, as the United States defeated France 2–0, brought her the 80th shutout, a record for an American goalkeeper.

The women on the U.S. national team have said that nothing makes them feel more confident than knowing that Solo is defending their goal. She is powerful, nothing escapes her attention, and she never gives up.

Solo has made many errors in her life, as she readily admits. "I want people to realize I'm just human and I make mistakes," she said. "And I want people to be able to forgive me."

ABBY WAMBACH
STRIKER
UNITED STATES

BORN JUNE 2, 1980
IN ROCHESTER, NEW YORK,
UNITED STATES
HEIGHT 5'11"
CURRENT TEAM WESTERN
NEW YORK FLASH (USA)
INTERNATIONAL GAMES 233
GOALS 177

ABBY WAMBACH

The Enduring Warrior

When asked about Abby Wambach, the manager of the Icelandic women's national team, Freyr Alexandersson, was succinct: "In the box, Abby is a monster!" The words ring true. Ever since joining the U.S. national team, Wambach has racked up goals, and on a good day she is absolutely unstoppable. Wambach has broken almost all possible goal-scoring records, and when she scored four goals in a friendly against South Korea on June 20, 2013, she broke Mia Hamm's record of 158 goals as a member of the U.S. national team. Wambach is powerful, strong, and tall, and her headers are precise and her fighting spirit ever present. After her fantastic performance during the 2012 Olympics, Wambach was selected FIFA's World Player of the Year. She has accumulated countless honors and awards, but the Women's World Cup has remained out of reach.

Nowadays, Wambach rarely plays the entire match with her team, but by means of her power and determination, she is able to change the course of a game with fierce goals and meticulous assists.

When Wambach was asked on Twitter about her inspirations, she said, "The inability to know how far I can push myself: physically, mentally, and emotionally. I want to be an ambassador for the game, and to inspire young kids. But I also want to inspire myself to win a Women's World Cup final." When she was asked about her pregame rituals, she replied, "I have tons of rituals. But I can't tell you any of them. I'd love to . . . but I can't!"

Other titles in the World Soccer Legends series

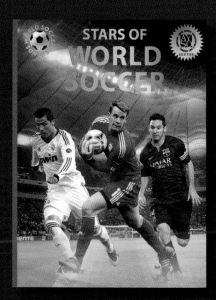

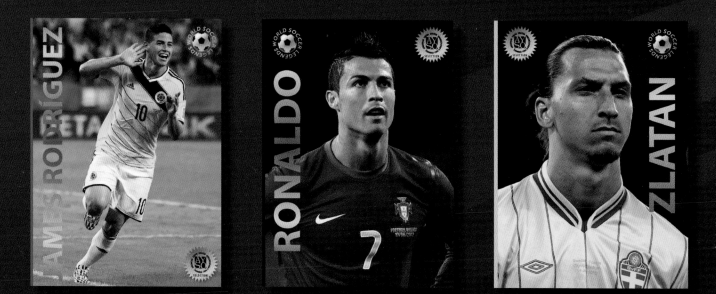